Contents

Introduction —   7

1   Design sketches   9

2   Figure drawing   10

3   Design sketching   22

4   Faces, hairstyles and hats   32

5   Pockets   43

6   Sleeves   46

7   Collars and neck lines   49

8   Drawing details   56

9   Production design drawing   64

10 Techniques   70

11 Presentation   86

Materials   94

Acknowledgments
I would like to thank Alan Hamp of Batsford for his generous help with some of the more technical aspects of this book. The Staff of the Library of the London College of Fashion were always helpful in aiding my research. Alexander Reissner deserves especial thanks for his unfailing help and encouragement.

Introduction

When working as a designer it is an advantage to be able to express your ideas on paper. The designer when sketching develops a style which in time becomes his 'handwriting'. It is good practice to start by sketching your ideas on paper, working on a series of adaptations, experimenting with design details and general effects.

There are many ways in which a designer will work at this stage. In this book a selection of styles and techniques is illustrated. For a beginner it is important to practise and experiment with techniques. You will then in time, discover that your own style of drawing develops. This will enable you to express your ideas with speed. It is a great advantage when working to acquire the ability to convey your ideas to others with the aid of a sketch.

1 Design sketches

The first technique illustrated has been developed for students who may find some difficulty in drawing and require a system that will enable them to express their ideas on paper with the use of a figure guide and the aid of semi-transparent paper.

The figures illustrated can be copied from the book or constructed from the proportions of heads into the body as illustrated (see pages 11–13).

It is good practise to make sketches from a garment, observing all the details, i.e. the shape of a lapel, the cut of a jacket, the placing of the pockets, etc. If possible it is useful to sketch the garment on a stand or from a model. If you are able to persuade someone to model a garment for you this will help your drawing considerably.

Fill your sketch books with observations of different fashion details. It is helpful to use a small sketch book. This is convenient for making sketches and fashion notes, when attending fashion shows, exhibitions and making general observations. A designer should always be aware of current fashions and the changes that are taking place. Fashion changes are created by many influences, e.g. music, films, theatre, travel and the events in society generally. This collection of sketches will prove to be a useful source later when designing.

A study and a knowledge of fabrics is essential for the designer. When designing for a specific market, activity or occasion, e.g. sports wear, industry, travel, etc., the correct materials selected for the design are important and require careful consideration.

Many new materials are being introduced with specific advantages. The introduction of new weaves, colours, patterns and textures give the designer a constant source of inspiration. It is a useful idea to keep a collection of small sample pieces of fabric for reference, make a note of any new fabrics that are being promoted each season.

2 Figure drawing

When constructing the figure, the basic figure proportion is eight heads tall. When sketching, the beginner should always sketch with light pencil lines, checking the correct proportions of the figure by using the method illustrated. The vertical or balance line must be drawn from the pit of the neck to the supporting foot to indicate that the head and the neck are above the supporting foot taking the weight of the figure.

It is useful to indicate the figure with a few lines before sketching the design. When designing the garment on the figure you will find it to be helpful to draw a line following the contour of the body (see pages 16–17).

It is important that a designer should be able to make a basic sketch of the figure when expressing ideas on paper. If possible it is an advantage to attend life classes and to make a study of anatomy. However, if this is not possible you can develop a technique of drawing the figure by following the illustrated methods suitable for producing design sketches.

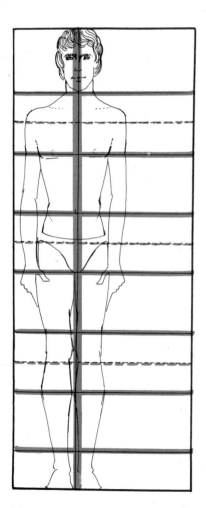

Right
Illustrated here are three basic poses of the male figure suitable for design drawing. When designing it is helpful to be able to sketch the figure from different angles. The figure need only be suggested with a few simple lines.

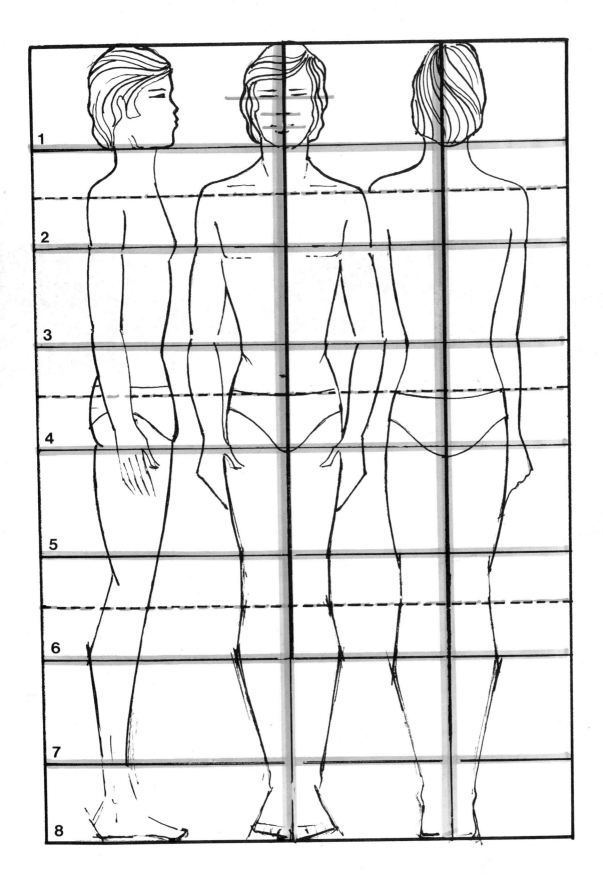

1
2
3
4
5
6
7
8

Note the construction of the two poses using the eight heads into the figure method.

Observe the guide lines indicated showing the position of the shoulders, hips and centre front line. When drawing and designing shirts, jackets, etc. it is not necessary to sketch the full length of the figure.

As an exercise, copy this pose using the method illustrated, then develop some variations of your own.

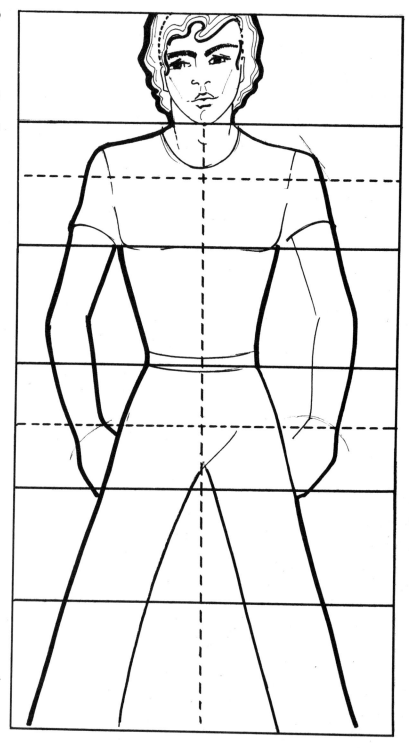

The centre front line follows the contour of the figure. This line is most useful when turning the figure, balancing a design and placing pockets, style features, etc.

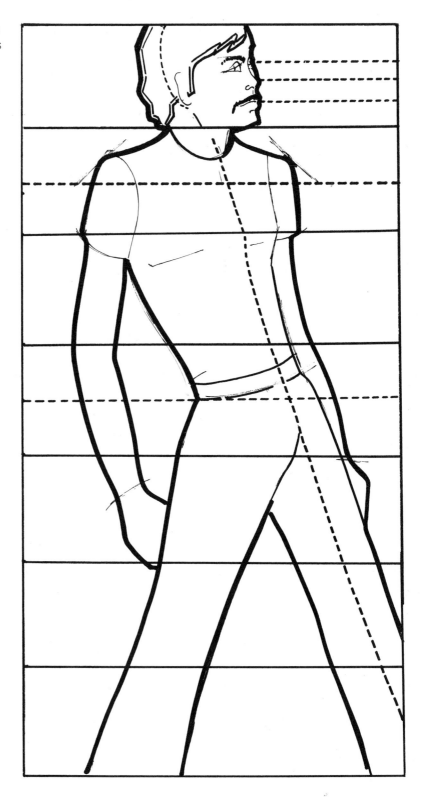

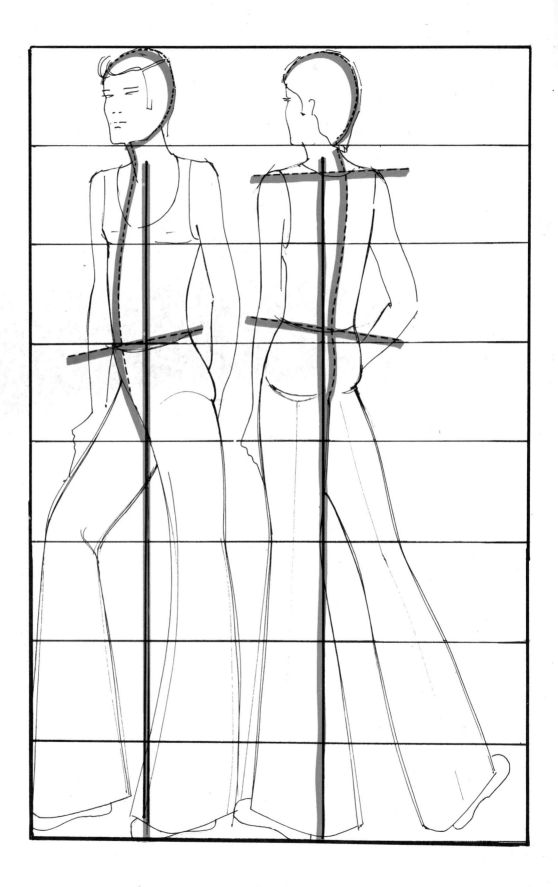

Experiment with the construction of the figures, developing different poses and giving the figures more movement. Note how the poses have been constructed. The coloured lines indicate the basic construction. The balance line falls from the pit of the neck to the foot taking the weight of the pose; the centre front line follows the contour of the figure.

These two developed poses illustrate a leisure outfit. The head, face, arms, and shoes are only indicated. One colour has been applied with a sable brush and water-colour paint.

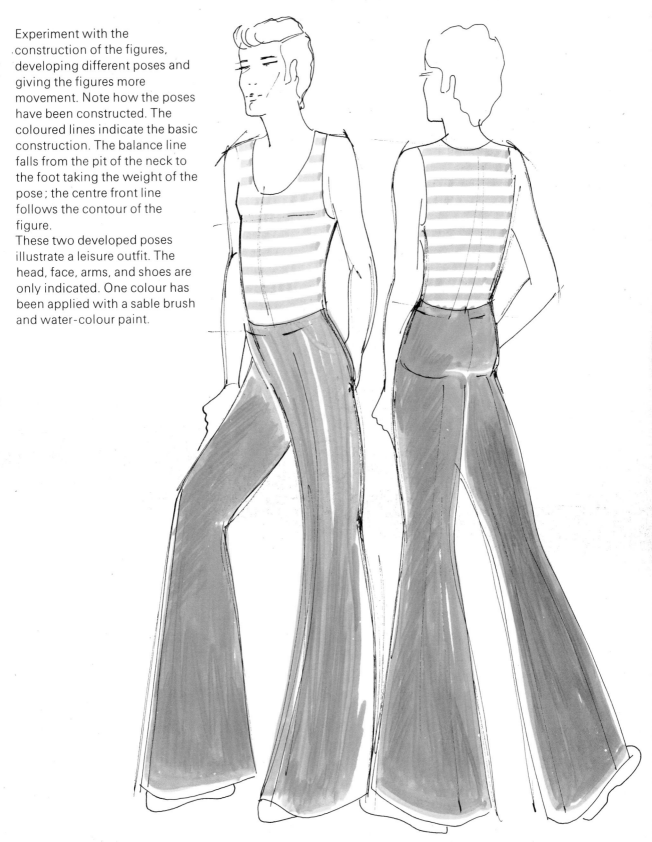

15

With practice you will gain confidence and develop a style of drawing of your own, but at first it is important to experiment as much as possible before developing your own style. Some students may have more ability in drawing than others, but in time and with practice an assured technique can be achieved.

The three figures illustrated on the left have been sketched with a free line, but figure proportions and basic construction have been observed.

The figures taken a stage further, illustrating a sports vest and casual trousers. Note how the sketch has been simplified in the second stage of working.

Keep a sketch book of figure drawings, practise working in different media — pen and ink, pencil, crayon, etc. Sketch when possible from life or photographs. The drawings need not be detailed, as these illustrations show.

Once you have achieved a number of suitable figure poses on which to design, you will find it possible to adapt the figure into other positions.

19

Three stages of the
development of a design
drawing illustrating a
leisure jacket:
1   The simple construction
of the figure.
2   Figure re-traced from
the original sketch
and simplified.
3   Design produced on the
figure. Note the careful
placing of pockets, buttons
and style features.

3 Design sketching

Design sketching and the development of your ideas should be expressed in a free and spontaneous way. For this a style of sketching should be developed which will enable the designer to create ideas and express them on paper.

When working on a collection of garments, the designs usually begin with a series of sketches working on a theme and experimenting with silhouettes, lines, patterns, textures and colours.

At this stage speed and clarity of line are important. In time and with practice the designer acquires a style which is often referred to as a designer's handwriting.

The design sketches can be produced on separate sheets of paper or a selection can be produced on one sheet. Detail notes together with a fabric sample should be added.

The purpose of this work apart from its use as a means of developing ideas is that it also helps to translate ideas to the design and production team with whom you could be working.

This is a very direct and clear way of expressing your ideas to others.

There exist many styles in which one may express these ideas on paper. Should it be found to be difficult in the first stages to produce the correct figure proportions, it helps to make some figure guides as shown (on pages 24–25).

This, with the aid of thin semi-transparent paper which is placed over the figure guide, will enable you to work on the impression of the underlying figure. (See page 28).

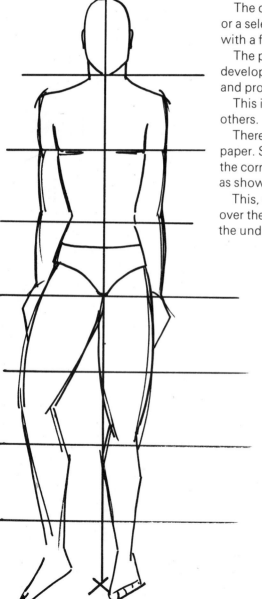

Right
Clear basic design drawing with back view indicated. This has been developed with the aid of a simple line drawing of the figure placed under transparent paper.
1   The garment designed and drawn over the figure guide.
2   Details added, buttons, pockets and stripes of the fabric. Two fibre-point pens of different thickness have been used for the general effects.

Three stages of producing a
design of a light-weight jacket:
1   The basic figure constructed
with the methods described in
chapter 1.
2   The figure retraced from the
original drawing and simplified.
3   The design developed on the
figure and completed in detail.
This is a simple and direct
method of working for
beginners.

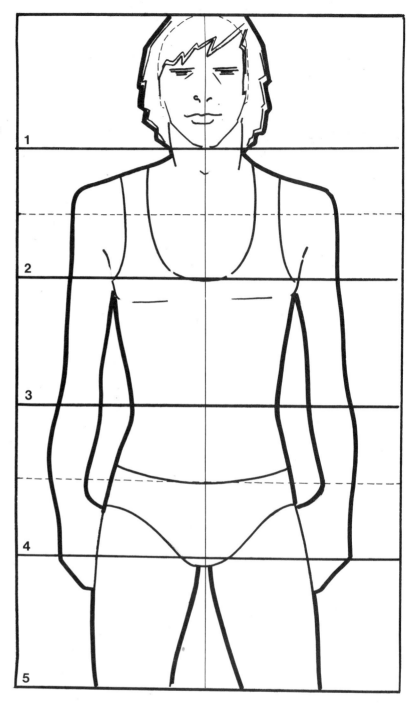

When designing and experimenting with an idea or theme, it is an advantage to arrange the sketches in a row as you proceed with creating designs. This enables you to compare the ideas and variations of the details. Note that the design has been produced on the same pose. This may be done free hand or by the use of a guide placed under transparent paper.

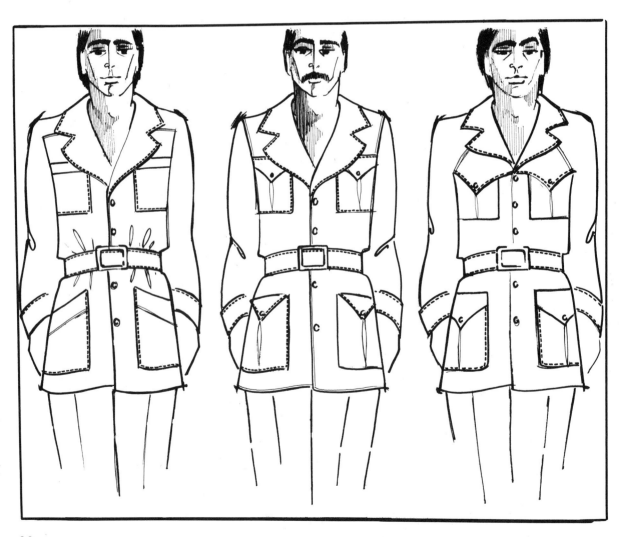

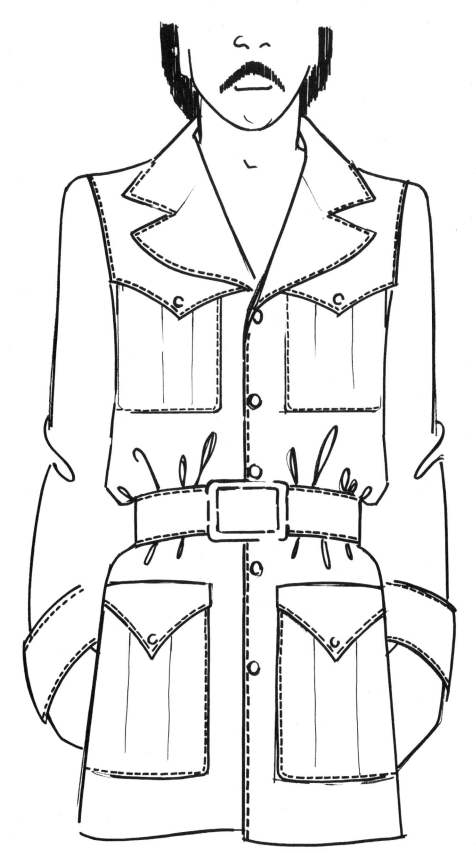

After gaining more experience, try to draw a figure in movement like the one illustrated This may be achieved by sketch ng the figure free hand, then working on the semi-transparent paper placed over the figure.

A sample sheet of designs
derived from the use of the
figure guide shown on the
opposite page – the sketches
were produced with a fine-
pointed pen. Note the free line
used. This technique requires
practice.

Two examples of design sheets showing front and back views. The pose has been produced from the figure guide produced on page 24. Note the clarity of the drawing and the care given to detail.

4 Faces, hairstyles and hats

The drawing of faces and hair styles need only be suggested in a design drawing. Often a stylized head is more effective than one that is too detailed. It is important to be able to construct the head with the correct proportions and the placing of the features. This can be done by various methods. Illustrated here are some simple techniques which you will find helpful. Work from the illustrations shown, try drawing from life and photographs and then work from imagination. When sketching it is not necessary to go into detail. The main points to observe are the shape, line and general direction of the hair. The effects of the layered cuts, waves, etc. need only be suggested.

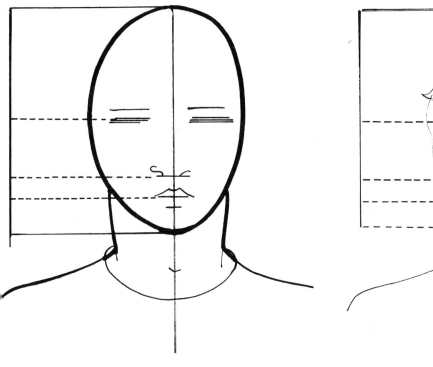

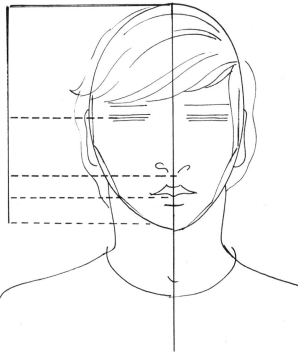

Three stages of constructing the head:
1 Sketch the oval shape of the head.
2 Work out the proportion of the placement of the features.
3 Outline the hair and develop the stylized techniques of representing the features and hair styles. Keep the details simple at this stage.

Make notes in your sketch book
of current fashion trends in hair
styles, beards and moustaches,
for reference.

Sketch faces from life or from
photographs in magazines.
Note the different features and
facial expressions. Practise
representing stylized drawings
of the head.
These stylized sketches were
produced with a felt pen on a
smooth white paper.

A selection of heads produced from photographs. They convey a feeling of life and imagination.

Note the different techniques in drawing, from very simple stylized drawings to the more detailed sketches. Make a selection of sketches in your sketch book, experiment with different pens and pencils, retrace your own drawings and make corrections.

Note the simple construction of the head produced from the oval shape divided up into sections and the effect of stylized features and hair.

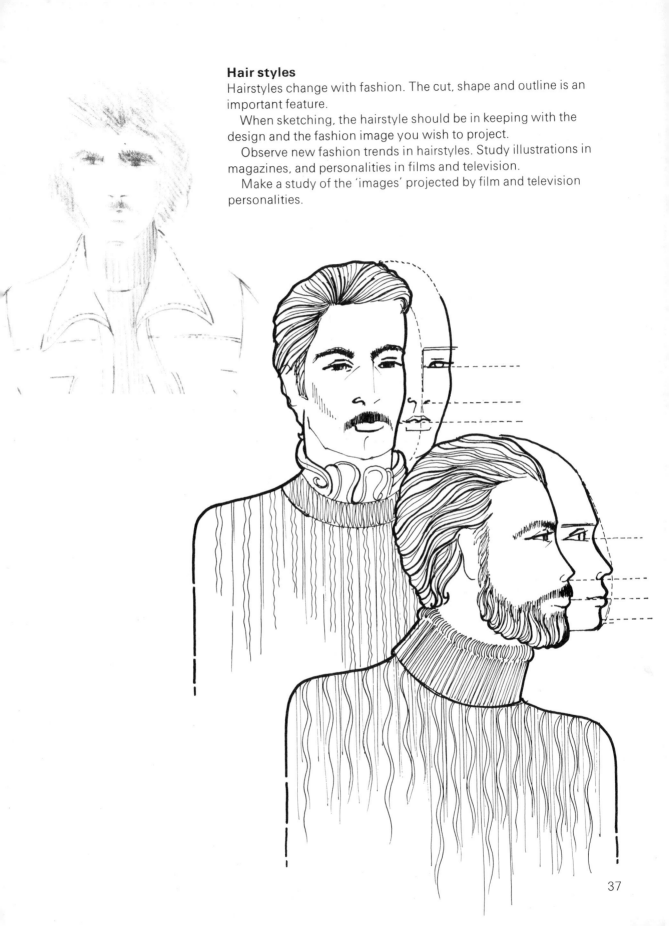

Hair styles

Hairstyles change with fashion. The cut, shape and outline is an important feature.

When sketching, the hairstyle should be in keeping with the design and the fashion image you wish to project.

Observe new fashion trends in hairstyles. Study illustrations in magazines, and personalities in films and television.

Make a study of the 'images' projected by film and television personalities.

Hats

When drawing and designing hats it is important to sketch the hat to fit on to the head and illustrated at the correct angle. Start by sketching the shape of the head in first. Use balance lines for the correct effect.

Sketch the correct shape you wish to express with a few lines only. As your ideas develop the sketches will reflect more confidence. Make a study of the current trends. Always keep a sketch book handy. Make sketches and notes of any new styles for future reference.

Note the construction of the head and the way in which the hat fits round the head. Keep the sketches light and simple in line suggesting the head and features.

Practise sketching different
shapes of hats, working from
photographs or a model. Note
the way the hat is worn. Sketch
the same hat from different
angles.

When designing and developing
ideas remember that the total
look or image depends on the
accessories and hair style as well
as the design of the garment.

5 Pockets

Pockets are an important design feature. There are many variations on a few basic styles, i.e. patch pockets, welt, jetted and seam, etc.

These may vary in style, with or without flaps, buttoned down flaps, and be of different shapes and sizes with style features incorporating pleats, tucks, top stitching, etc. They are decorative as well as being functional.

When designing, the shape and size of the pocket and placing should be considered carefully in relation to the general proportions and balance of the garment.

Practise sketching the different styles and create variations. Observe the use of pockets in fashion generally, make sketches from fashion magazines and observations from window displays.

Jetted pockets arranged at different angles.

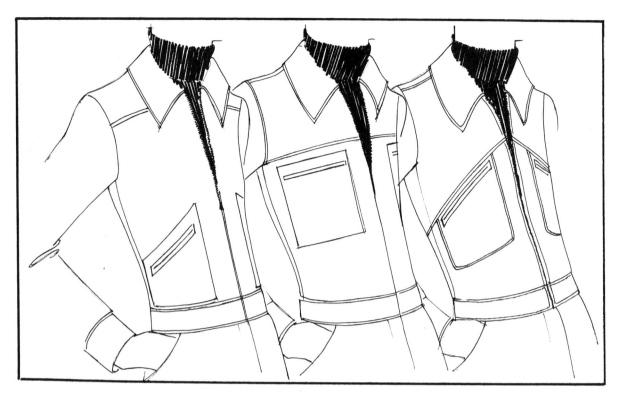

Patch pockets with zip opening.

Seam pockets with a stand.

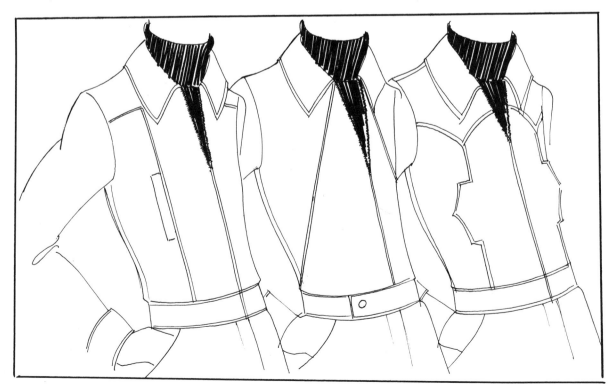

Design Exercise – Casual Sports Jacket

Occasion Summer walking
holiday in the country.
Fabric Light-weight cotton drill
(or own choice)
Colour Own choice.
Style Features Pockets and
seams with top stitching. Cuffs
and collars.

Practical design considerations
Functional design features
1   Placement of pockets for
easy availability, size and
number for containing maps,
etc.
2   Openings and type of
fasteners for easy adjustment in
changing weather conditions.
3   Cut and seam placement for
easy movement.
4   Colour and type of fabric
considering weather conditions,
weight while walking and
general maintenance.

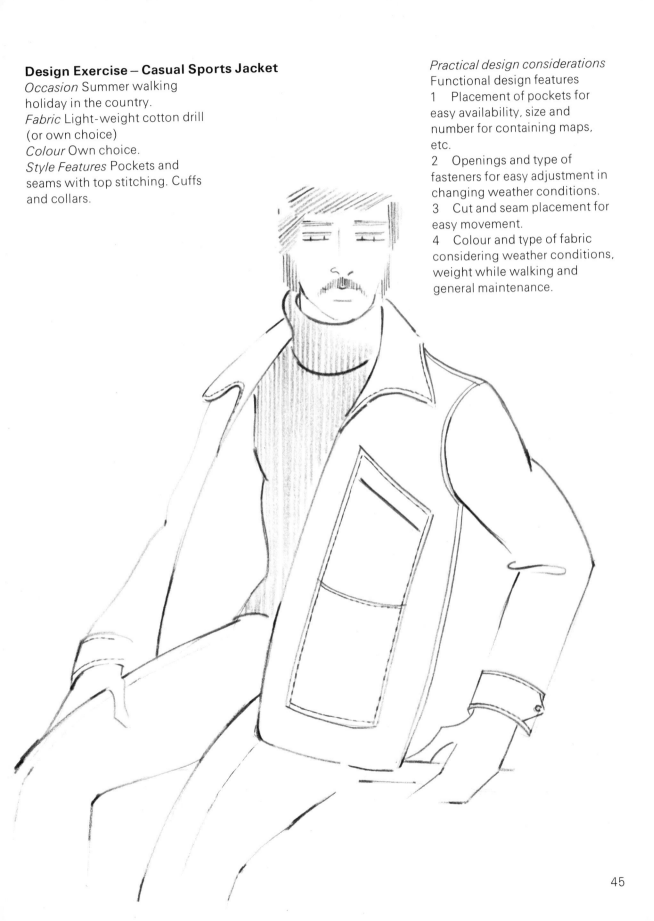

6 Sleeves

There exist many variations of the sleeve. In fashion the sleeve is a very important feature. There are a few basic styles with many adaptations: the set-in sleeve with variations of armhole shapes; the Raglan sleeve cut high or low; and the sleeve cut in one with the body and known as the Kimono sleeve (see illustrations).

Designers of fashion for menswear use many sleeve variations and are breaking away from the conventional classic styles. Different fashion trends and a more casual style of dressing for certain occasions have been introduced.

Make observations of the many different sleeve variations and the way in which they have been used related to the complete balance of a design; also the practical aspects of the sleeve design considering the activity for which the garment would be worn.

When sketching the sleeve make sure you achieve correct style in the drawing considering the cut and changing shape which has been designed round the arm.

left Saddle sleeve
right Raglan

left   Kimono sleeve
right Set-in sleeve.

Keep your sketch book up to date, noting any new style of sleeve.
    Consider the possibilities of the sleeve as a feature in a design from cuff interest to the general shape and cut.
    The design of sleeves for tailored jackets to the more casual jacket, shirts and knitwear requires special consideration.

Design and Drawing Exercise

Design a collection of casual jackets for a young market, suggesting two materials, one plain and one patterned, introducing the sleeve style as a feature.

Design Casual Jacket
Season Autumn
Market Young market
Occasion For leisure wear suitable for general use—smart and casual
Style features Design of sleeve and collar
Fabrics Own choice in two contrasting colours one plain, one patterned (reflecting current fashion colours)
Image Casual - smart

Practical Design Considerations

Fabrics Type of fabric for warmth, general wear and maintenance
Movement Cut and designed for comfort and easy movement
Fasteners Easy to open and adjust suitable for general use — smart
Pockets General use and placement
Collars Adaptable to weather conditions

Work using the figure guide or work free hand. Note the arrangement and how the ideas have been evolved, using the one pose to develop the ideas.

48

7 Collars and neck lines

Collars and neck lines in menswear design change with fashion in shape and style. There are many variations. As with pockets and sleeves the variations are derived from the basic styles. Fashion trends vary from narrow to wide collars and revers of various shapes and sizes. The many variations of the collar, with a stand and polo necks, crew- and V-shape necks, continually return in fashion.

When sketching the collar take care to achieve the correct look you require, noting the way the collar is balanced and fits round the neck and lies on the shoulders.

Note the way in which the collar and lapels have been drawn. It is very important to get the correct balance of the collar and lapel in your sketch. You will find a few guide lines when working will help considerably. (see pages 54 and 55)

Exercise – Design and Draw
As an exercise, sketch the same figure (head and shoulders) and design a collar and lapel four times, introducing different shapes. (See page 50)

Sketch book reference

Keep a record of different collars and fashion styles in your sketch book. Note the way in which they are cut and the name and type of garment on which the collar is designed.

Illustrated are three collars sketched from current fashion leisure garments. Collect from old magazines and fashion articles and advertisements drawings or photographs of sleeves, pockets or collars for your reference.

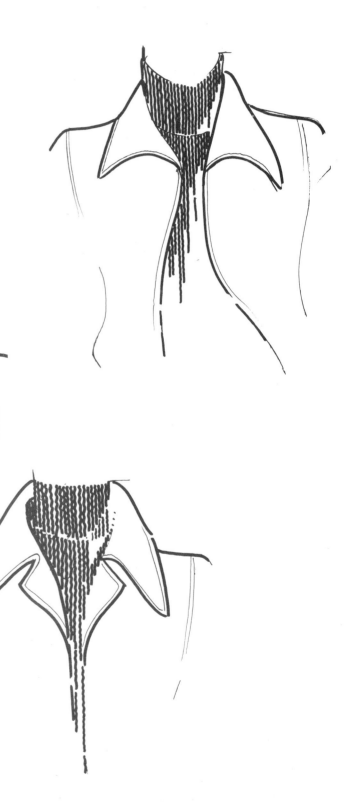

Single-breasted button-fastening

When drawing and balancing the single-breasted fastening make sure the buttons are placed on the centre front line. Note in the illustrations the use of the guide lines. These will help to ensure you achieve the correct balance.

Practice sketching the double-and single-breasted fastenings as shown in the two stages.

8 Drawing details

Practise drawing the details of garments. Study photographs illustrating pleating, collars, sleeves, yokes and style features. Note the way in which they have been made, and the different effects achieved within a design. It is good practice to make sketches from a garment, observing all the details, e.g. the shape of a lapel and the cut of a jacket, to the placing of the buttons and pockets, etc. Fill your sketch books with observations of the many different details. It is best to use a small sketch book for this purpose as it can more easily be carried about for making fashion notes and sketches.

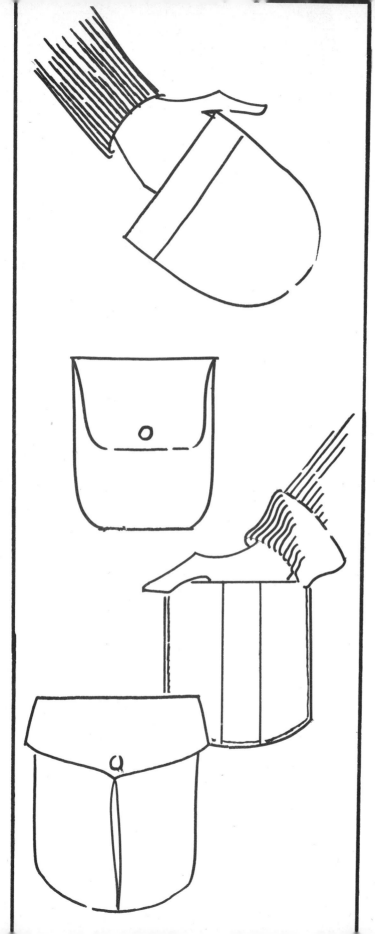

A selection of patch pockets.

These are pockets which are applied to the right side of the material. There are many shapes and variations. Illustrated are a few styles. Make sketches from your own garments of the pocket detail noting the shape and general effects.

Right
Yokes and Seams
Note the many variations of the details of the garments.

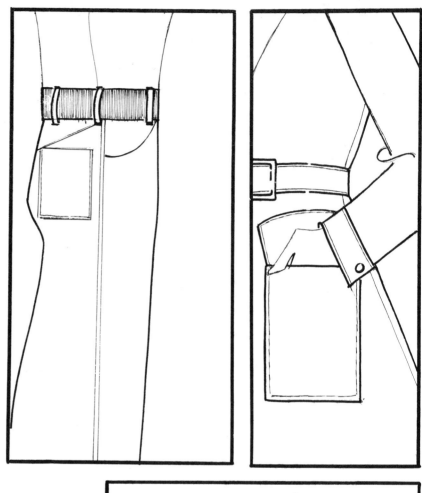

Observe the details of a garment when sketching, making notes on the general behaviour of the different materials and the way in which they hang and fall into folds. Note also the many variations of the collar, sleeve, and pockets. It is good practice to make sketches of them from different angles. Study the way designers are introducing style features into fashion.

Study a section of a garment
and draw the details with care,
noting the placement of seams,
pockets, collars, etc. related to
the general balance of the
design.

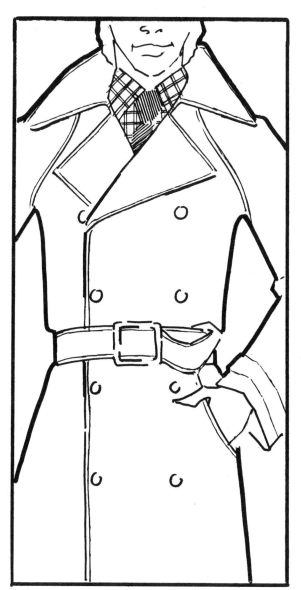

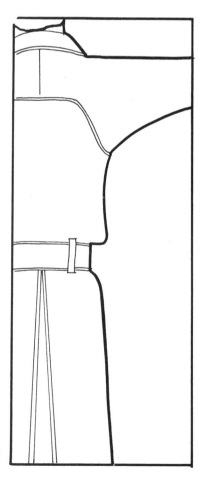

Sketch back views of garments
noting the placement of the
details.

9 Production design drawing

The production drawing must be clear in every detail, relating the design to the average proportions of the figure. The drawing is usually a flat one clearly giving the correct information the production team and pattern cutter would require.

The drawing is an analysis of the fashion sketch. The practical aspects of the design would be considered, e.g. the cut of the garment in relation to the figure, the type of fastening, collar, sleeves, etc. and the placing of the seams.

A back view of the design is also required with all details shown. Should the design have any intricate detail this should be drawn separately. Detailed notes would be added with full information on the garment. Fabric and accessories to be used, e.g. threads, fastenings, linings, etc. should also be given.

Clear diagrammatic drawings are necessary for production or working sketches. Remember to relate all details to the figure, considering the shape, cut and placing of style lines and general features.

Draw a few basic figure shapes suitable for this type of work which you could use when working (see illustrations).

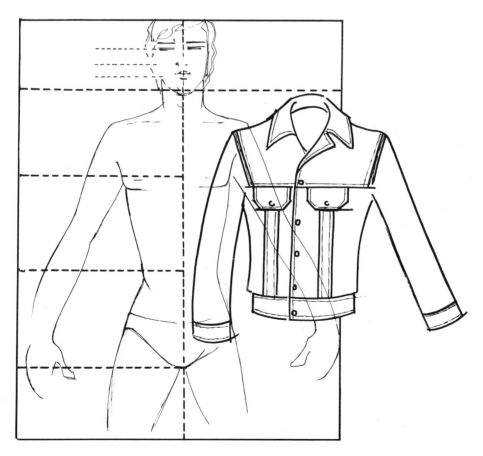

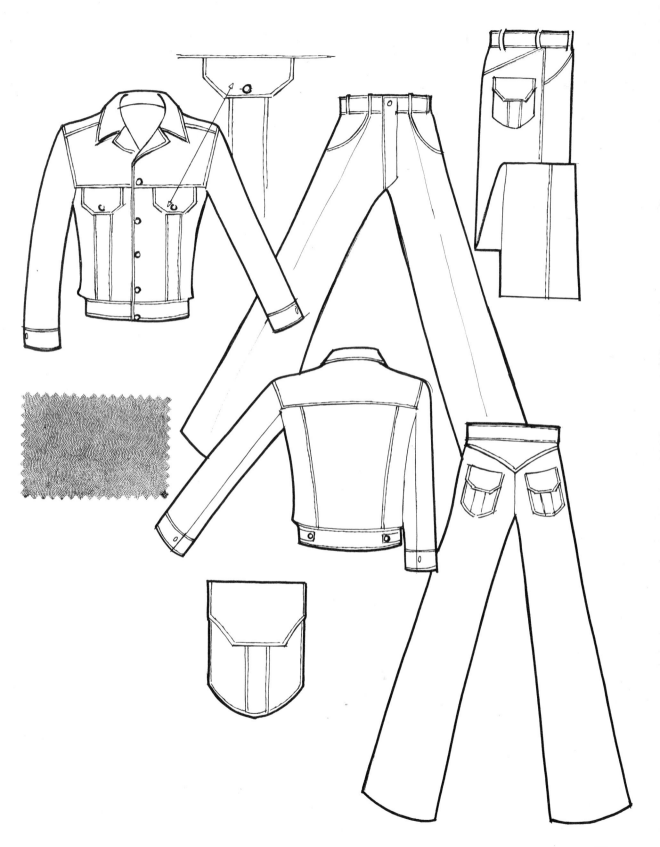

The development of the
production drawing. Note the
way in which all the details have
been drawn. For this style of
drawing the details of the head,
hands and feet are not shown.

Clear diagrammatic sketches
working over a basic figure
guide with semi-transparent
paper. For this style of
production sketch the
proportions of the figure must
be related to the design. A fibre-
point pen has been used to
produce a clear bold line, and
the fine details drawn in with a
drawing pen.

Production sketch, giving full details of the design. Note the balance of the collar, pockets and button placement. The detail notes would also be shown on this sheet together with a sample of the fabric.

Examples of production drawings for a coat, illustrating front and back views as diagrammatic drawings.

10 Techniques

The techniques of producing a design sketch vary considerably. Many effects may be achieved by the use of different media. For a beginner it is important to experiment as much as possible by working in pencil, chalk, pastel, pen and ink, crayon, etc. It is good practice to draw the same design several times, using a different pencil, pen or crayon. You will be surprised at the different effects that follow on the same basic drawing. On page 94 there is a list of materials you will find helpful when experimenting with techniques. They range from the basic simple materials to the more sophisticated pens, etc.

Materials Used

In the illustration on the opposite page the drawing method incorporates a number of different pens and pencils to attain the various textures and line values.

Rain Coat   Fibre-point pen with grey wash.

Pullover   Dark grey wash with ribbed effect produced with a fine pen.

Tweed Trousers   Grey water-colour paint and black crayon pencil with a fine point.

Scarf   Black wax crayon

Check Shirt   Fine pen and ink

Head and Face   Pen and ink with a soft pencil for shading of the hair.

Note the three stages of this sketch:
1   The design has been sketched with light lines.
2   The development using sharper lines in the drawing where detail will be emphasized.
3   The sketch completed with the ribbed effect of the cardigan and sweater on the collar, belt, pockets and cuffs. This effect was obtained by using a fine fibre-tipped pen with a line technique as illustrated.

Three stages showing the development of a design sketch. Note the position of the figure and the style details of the jacket and waist band of the trousers.

The drawing has been done with the use of a drawing pen: Number 5. The final stage illustrates the patterned shirt and suede texture of the jacket with elasticated waist band and cuffs, painted with water-colour paint.

Textures

Practise developing different textures of various media. Note the weave of a fabric or the stitching effects of knitwear and the behaviour of material when cut and made up in certain ways, e.g. leather, suede, knitwear, fur, etc. Keep a note in your sketch books of the ways in which a certain effect has been achieved. By experimenting, you will discover many techniques which you can later use when working on your design drawings.

Pullover Fibre-point pen with irregular line.
Herringbone Tweed Fine Pen nib and black ink.
Check shirt Pen and ink. Note the use of the pattern to illustrate the way in which the shirt is cut.

Experiment
Take a collection of felt-tipped
pens of varying thicknesses and
experiment to achieve the effect
of various textures, patterns and
line values as illustrated.

77

Three stages, illustrating a presentation design sketch of a casual sports outfit:

1   Sketch drawn lightly. Note the use of the construction lines to achieve the correct balance of the figure.

2   Style details drawn in and the pattern of the shirt emphasized.

3   The final effect has been given by the use of a half-tone grey wash.

This sketch has been produced with the use of a light pencil line sketched over in ink, using a medium-sized drawing pen. The water-colour wash has been added. When painting over ink make sure you are using a waterproof ink or fibre-point pen, or the ink will run.

These different effects have been made with: Fibre-point pens of different sizes; drawing pens; and black water-colour paint with a sable brush, size 6.

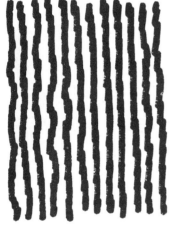

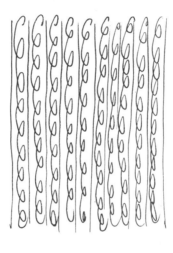

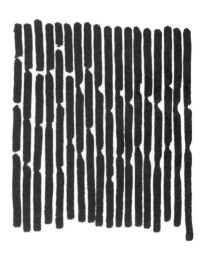

Felt pens of various thicknesses incorporated in the one drawing, using the pen and line value with different techniques.

Pen and Ink drawings

. . . using different line values to achieve the effects of knitwear and patterned shirts and trousers. Note the same pose illustrating the development of the designs in line, thus enabling the designer to compare the ideas as they emerge.

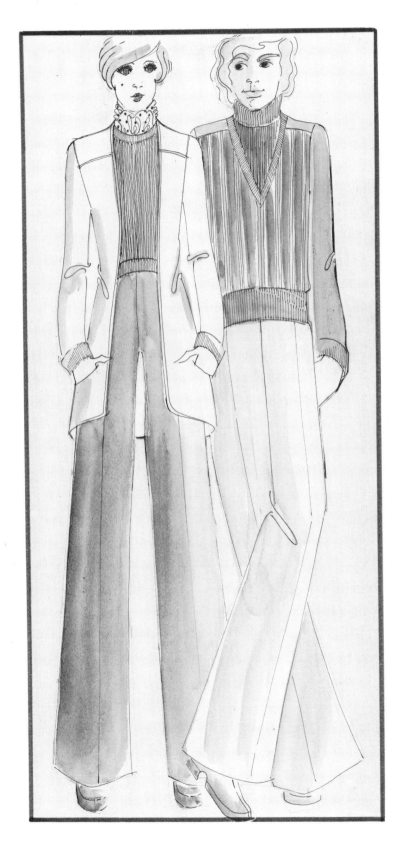

Pen-and-ink sketches with grey water-colour wash added. Note the effects of shadow and light achieved with the colour wash.

Pencils

Practise drawing with different pencils of various thicknesses using a variety of soft and hard leads. By the pressure of the line when working varied effects may be produced. Note the use of the pencil and the textures achieved, as seen in these drawings.

11 Presentation

The presentation of design work is very important when attending an interview or showing your work to clients, buyers, and entering for competitions and general display for assessment.

A large selection of papers and cards are available and these can be used according to the effects you require. For a simple presentation when the work is to be handled frequently it is a good idea to protect it in a transparent folder. These folders are obtainable in various sizes. They are a good investment for a student as the design work may be replaced and the folders used again.

For competitions and display purposes mounts cut in card will help the presentation considerably. The mounts would be cut with the aid of a sharp knife and a rule. A certain skill is required when cutting the mount which can be acquired with care and practice. Illustrated in this chapter are different ways in which to mount the work and suggested layouts for the design drawings and general effects. The selection of drawing paper and coloured card is considerable. The prices vary according to the quality and thickness of the card.

When adding lettering to the presentation it is an advantage if you are able to produce a good standard of lettering. If you should not have acquired the skill the use of a stencil set, typewriter or transfer lettering is helpful and effective. This last method, however, you will find to be expensive for a student's budget.

Main considerations when presenting work are:

1   The general style of drawing and the media used, e.g. pen, ink, paint, pastel, etc.
2   The arrangement of the figures, the front and back views. The back views of garments can be drawn on a figure or can be drawn flat (see page 62) : which would depend on the design and the details to be shown. A side view is sometimes required when a design feature is shown on a sleeve, trouser or jacket.

The figures may be arranged on a sheet in a group or a single figure with a diagrammatic back view. In some instances it is not necessary to draw the figure full length when presenting a jacket, coat or shirt, etc. (see page 68)

3   The notes should clearly give all the necessary information. It is good practice to arrange your notes in a neat block. Fabric samples suggesting the material used should be attached to the sheet. These need only be small, not more than 1 in.
4   When selecting your card for mounting the work, consider with care the colour and texture of the card which will complement the design drawing.
5   The general display effects of your work. Simple background sketches and use of colour.
6   Should you work on a collection of drawings for either a client, buyer or assessment for an examination it is advisable to keep to a standard size.

This will make it easier for the client or examiner to look through your work.
It is also advisable to keep your work flat in a folder. Never roll your sketches, particularly when you wish to show them.

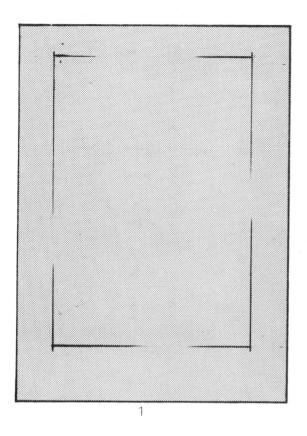

1

2

1   Card with window of frame drawn in light pencil lines on the facing side of the card.
2   The frame cut out with a sharp cutting blade. When cutting the knife should be held at an angle to achieve a bevelled edge.
3   The design sheet placed at the back of the mount and fastened with tape.
4   *Right,* work complete for presentation. Notice, to give a pleasing balance the frame has more space at the bottom.

A simple method of cutting without the effect of a bevelled edge can be achieved by drawing the frame on the reverse side of the card and by scoring the line with blade and rule.

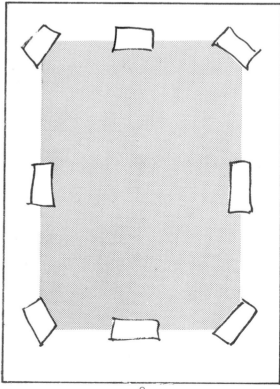

3

Flat mounting by placing the drawing on the card and fixing with an adhesive spray. Make sure the drawing is straight and clean cut on the edges. Detail notes and sample fabrics can be displayed on the design sketch or on the frame.

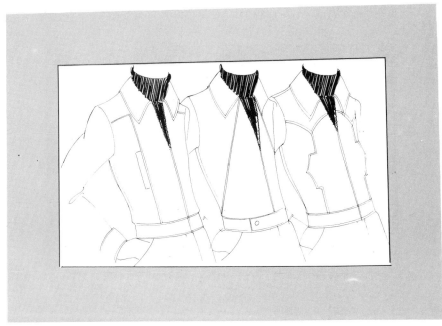

Materials

Fashion boards   High quality board extra thick will take charcoal, crayon, gouache, tempera and water-colour paints.

Water-colour boards   Saunders Water Colour Boards prepared from a mould-made paper. The paper has an even surface.

Bristol board   The board has a high rag content with a fine white surface. Ideal for pen and ink work.

Pasteboard   An inexpensive white board for paste-up and general studio use.

Illustration boards   A board with a smooth surface which will take ink, crayon, pencil, wash or colour. Produced in different sizes.

Cartridge paper   White paper with a finely grained surface suitable for pencil, crayon and colour. This paper is made in different thicknesses and quality.

Coloured cartridge paper   The surface has a slight texture. Suitable for colour work. Will take water colour and pastels.

Cartridge pads   Obtainable in a range of sizes with a stiff cardboard back.

Lay-out pads   White lay-out detail paper with a surface ideal for ink and pencil. Usually glued at top to strong cardboard back. Available in different sizes.

Ingres paper   The surface of this paper is ideal for pastel and tempera work. Good selection of colours.

Coloured tissue papers   Unglazed tissue paper, available in a large range of colours, is used in studios to produce inexpensive colour effects. The paper can be stuck to board or paper surfaces with Cow gum or adhesive spray.

Tracing paper and pads   Obtainable in sheets of different sizes or pads.

Herculene tracing film   Polyester film of good quality. Will take pencil and ink, ideal for photo copying and also colour separation work. May also be used for the protection of visual work.

Permatrace   Film with excellent drawing surface for ink and pencil. This film is virtually indestructible.

Tracing cloth   Good quality tracing cloth for work that must withstand considerable handling and wear.

Detail paper   A white paper with a high degree of transparency. Suitable when working from original roughs.

Pencils

A large selection of pencils is obtainable; the type of pencil used would depend on the effect required.

Pencils (wood cased)   The degree of hardness is printed on each pencil:

    6B is very soft. 9H very hard
    F and HB are medium
    EX is extremely soft.

Stabilo pencils   This pencil will write on any surface: film, glossy photographs, metals, etc.

Charcoal pencils   Gives the same effect as pure charcoal sticks. Made in hard, medium or soft qualities.

Carbon pencils   This pencil will produce a dull matt finish.

Black pencils   Heavy extra large leads for bold drawings in matt jet black.

Coloured pencils   A large variety of makes is available with a good range of colours.

Chinagraph (wax based)   This pencil is impervious to water and dampness, but it is possible to remove with a dry cloth.

Pens

A large selection of pens is available; listed are some chosen for the different effects that may be achieved.

Rapidograph pens   Technical pens that provide a means of drawing without the aid of constant refilling. The drawing point may be replaced with different sizes. Many pleasing effects may be obtained with the use of this pen, and also in combination with others.

Osmiroid fountain pens   A pen for lettering and script writing. A large range of interchangeable screw-in nibs (not suitable with Indian ink).

Technos drawing pen   The Pelikan Technos is a cartridge-filled drawing pen. Pen points are designed for different jobs, e.g.

ruling, stencilling, and free hand. Many interchangeable points are available.

Osmiroid Sketch fountain pen A very versatile sketching pen which provides a wide variety of line thickness from bold to a fine outline. This pen is fitted with a reservoir to maintain a constant ink flow. Indian ink should not be used.

Pen holders Many very simple wood or plastic pen holders with nibs are obtainable at a small cost.

A large selection of paints of varying qualities are manufactured:

    Watercolours
Designer Colours
    Poster Paints
Tubes of Oil Paint.

Pastels Pastels vary depending on the quality.

Coloured inks A large selection of coloured inks are available, some of which are waterproof.

Brushes Brushes are made in many sizes and qualities (sable, hog and squirrel hair).

Transparent acetate sheet Cellulose acetate film. Suitable for covering art work and presentation.

Presentation books Fitted with clear acetate pockets, ideal for presentation of work—photographs, drawings, etc.

Portfolios Strong durable portfolios in different sizes for storing art work.

Leathercloth portfolios Ideal for the protection of art work and carrying. Fitted with handle, two fasteners and a centre lock and key. Made in different sizes.

Stanley knife A craft knife with replaceable blades, ideal for cutting thick paper, heavy card, plastics, etc.

Swivel-head knives Cuts irregular curves, may be locked for straight lines.

Double-sided adhesive tape Suitable for quick mounting. Adhesive on both sides.

Protective sprays Spray to protect art work against damage—obtainable in gloss or matt.

Adhesive in aerosol cans Spray adhesive—colourless and water repellant. Will stick cloth, board, paper.

Cow gum Transparent rubber solution suitable for pasting work up. Sold in tins or tubes.

Copydex Very strong latex adhesive, may be used with paper and fabric.

Gum eraser or paper cleaner A soft pliable eraser gum. Suitable for cleaning art work. Will not damage the surface of the paper.

Kneaded eraser A putty rubber that can be moulded to the shape required.

Staedtler Mars plastic For use on drafting film, tracing cloth or paper.

Soft eraser A white soft eraser for soft lead.

Masking tape Tape seals with light pressure, with a water-repellant back.

Drafting tape Designed to hold film or paper to a drawing board and removed without damage. A very thin, adhesive crepe paper tape.

Light box A box with a glass top containing a light, used for tracing. By placing the work to be traced on a piece of transparent paper which lays on the glass and is illuminated underneath by the light the work is thrown into clear outline. These boxes are available in a range of sizes or can be quite easily constructed with even the most rudimentary knowledge of carpentry.

Editor's shears Paper shears with sharp point.

Transpaseal Flexible sheet of thin transparent plastic coated with a pressure-sensitive adhesive, obtainable in clear gloss or matt finish. Suitable for covering art work.

Drawing stands A varied selection are available made of wood and metal, in different sizes. The board can be adjusted according to the angle required.

Plan chest A chest designed to store drawings and large sheets of paper and card. Available in different units of drawers and sizes.

Air brush The air brush provides perfectly even tones, graded tints and soft lines, also the blending of colours. Operated by a motor compressor or compressed air propellant aerosols.